Election and Predestination

by

W.B. Godbey

First Fruits Press
Wilmore,
Kentucky c2017

Election and predestination. By W.B. Godbey.

First Fruits Press, © 2017

ISBN: 9781621717348 (print) 9781621717331 (digital), 9781621717362 (kindle)

Digital version at http://place.asburyseminary.edu/godbey/7/

First Fruits Press is a digital imprint of the Asbury Theological Seminary, B.L. Fisher Library. Asbury Theological Seminary is the legal owner of the material previously published by the Pentecostal Publishing Co. and reserves the right to release new editions of this material as well as new material produced by Asbury Theological Seminary. Its publications are available for noncommercial and educational uses, such as research, teaching and private study. First Fruits Press has licensed the digital version of this work under the Creative Commons Attribution Noncommercial 3.0 United States License. To view a copy of this license, visit http://creativecommons.org/licenses/by-nc/3.0/us/.

For all other uses, contact:

First Fruits Press
B.L. Fisher Library
Asbury Theological Seminary
204 N. Lexington Ave.
Wilmore, KY 40390
http://place.asburyseminary.edu/firstfruits

Godbey, W. B. (William Baxter), 1833-1920.
   Election and predestination / W.B. Godbey. – Wilmore, KY : First Fruits Press, ©2017.
   56 pages ; cm.
   Reprint. Previously published: Nashville, Tennessee : Pentecostal Mission Publishing Company, [190-?].
   ISBN: 9781621717348 (pbk.)
   1. Election (Theology) 2. Predestination. I. Title.
BT810.G62 2017   234

Cover design by Jon Ramsey

asburyseminary.edu
800.2ASBURY
204 North Lexington Avenue
Wilmore, Kentucky 40390

First Fruits Press
The Academic Open Press of Asbury Theological Seminary
204 N. Lexington Ave., Wilmore, KY 40390
859-858-2236
first.fruits@asburyseminary.edu
asbury.to/firstfruits

Election and Predestination

BY

W. B. GODBEY

PRICE 10 CENTS

PENTECOSTAL MISSION PUB. CO.
125 FOURTH AVENUE, NORTH
NASHVILLE. TENN.
U. S. A

HELPFUL BOOKS

SANCTIFICATION

	Cloth	Paper
Wholly Sanctified, by J. O. McClurkan	.40	.20
How to Keep Sanctified "		.05
Why Teach Holiness, Jas. M. Taylor		.1C
God's Provision for Holiness, N. J. Holmes	.50	.15
Scriptural Sanctification, P. R. Nugent		.05
The Secret of Spiritual Power, A. M. Hills	.50	.15
Facts, Faith and Fire, B. F. Haynes		.25
The Sanctified Life, "		.15
Holiness: Not a Modern Fad, By A. M. Hills		.05
Sanctification: What it is, How Obtained and How Retained, Sundry Authors	.40	.10
By His Life, M. H. Houston	.50	
Perfect Love, S. L. C. Coward		.05
God's Nazarite, W. B. Godbey		.10
Plain Account of Christian Perfection, Wesley		.10

SECOND COMING

Behold, He Cometh! J. O. McClurkan	.50	.25
Signs of His Coming, W. B. Godbey		.10
An Appeal to Postmillennialists, Godbey		.10
The Christhood and the Antichristhood, Godbey		.10
The Lord's Coming, C. H. M.		.10
The Millennium, W. B. Godbey		.10
The Age to Come, G. D. Watson		.25

BIOGRAPHY

Life of Samuel Rutherford, Henrietta Matson		.10
" " George Mueller " "		.10
Celebrated Missionaries, " "		.10
Recollections of Chas. G. Finney " "	.50	.20
Life of Madame Guyon, " "	.50	.10
Chosen Vessels, Sundry Authors	.50	.25

Pentecostal Mission Publishing Company
Nashville, Tenn.

Election and Predestination

W. B. GODBEY

PRICE 10 CENTS

Pentecostal Mission Publishing Company
Nashville, Tennessee.

ELECTION AND PREDESTINATION

From ages immemorial antipodal dogmatisms have universally prevailed, *i. e.*, God's sovereignty and man's free-agency; the former culminating in absolute fatalism as taught by the stoic philosophers of Greece and adopted by Mohammed in his Koran, the latter finding its *ultima thule* in reckless liberalism, developing into that ultra pantheism which makes every man a god. As in controversial matters generally, the truth abides in the interim between two errors; therefore, we conclude the divine sovereignty and human freedom are both incontestable verities, perfectly harmonical either with other, despite the incompetency of finite minds always to reconcile them. Election is from *ekout* and *legoo*, to choose. Predestination is from *pre*, beforehand, and *destinal*, to a point, hence it means an antecedent appointment.

CHAPTER I.

PHARAOH.

Rom. 9:17, for says the Scripture to Pharaoh, "Unto this very thing have I raised thee up, in order that I may show forth my power in thee and in order that my name may be proclaimed in all the earth." The *vox-populi* raises the lugubrious howl, "Poor old Pharaoh!" Plagued by ten awful castigatory judgments sent on him by the great Jehovah because he would not let Israel go. These terrible righteous retributions desolated his country over and over, sweeping away the super-abounding products of that garden of the world, destroying herds and flocks almost indiscriminately, and finally slaying the first-born in every home, precipitating the people into insurgency by their unanimous clamors constraining him to let Israel go lest their God slay every one of them.

After the long, heated controversy culminating in their emancipation, the awful infatuation of the haughty autocrat, superinduced by the hardening of his heart, which they impute to divine intervention, constrains him to rise up with his army and pursue his fugitive slaves with all possible expedition. Overtaking them at the expiration of three days, confronted by the sea, hemmed in right and left by Pihahiroth and Baal-zepher, impassable mountains, he is in the act of recapturing them all, when they unanimously clamor against Moses, "Were there no graves in Egypt that you have brought us away here to perish by the sword of Pharaoh and leave our bones to bleach on the naked shore?" Moses responds, "Stand still and see the salvation of the Lord." Then he walks out in front of the host, smites the sea with his old shepherd's staff, now paradoxically prolific of miracles, and splits it from shore to shore, thus opening the way of escape from the triumhpant army of the infuriated king. The pillar of cloud by day and fire by night which led them out of Egypt now moves to the rear, the front luminous as meridian day, and the rear black as midnight, flooding the Egyptians with dismal darkness, while Israel enjoys superabounding light. The Egyptian army, heroically pursuing them, thinking they had found a way of escape overland, come down into the bed of the sea. Now, the hosts of Israel shout the victory, safe on the Asiatic shore, led by Miriam, the preaching sister of Moses; meanwhile the leader of Israel stretches forth his staff toward the sea, when, responsive to his bidding, the floods collapse, wrapping the Egyptians in watery winding sheets. How sad the doom of poor old Pharaoh! his country desolated, his slaves all emancipated, and himself, with his royal army, not only drowned in the depths of the

ELECTION AND PREDESTINATION. 7

sea, but lost in the abyss of irretrievable doom, sadly verifying the proclamation, "Those who do not reign in righteousness shall perish from the earth." Such is the popular interpretation of the preceding Scripture appertaining to Pharaoh, but, like carloads of Biblical exegesis, utterly untrue.

(a) As to God's hardening Pharaoh's heart, we may simply observe, the same sunshine softens the wax and hardens the clay. In a similar manner the glorious Sun of Righteousness pouring down the effulgence of His everlasting Gospel on all the people in the world, softens those who yield, and hardens those who reject, verifying His word—the Gospel "a savor of life unto life and of death unto death." The exegesis of this wonderful Scripture appertaining to Pharaoh is simple and beautiful. God had actually given him the sovereignty of the world. He was Rameses II, the celebrated Sesostris of history— the first man to conquer and rule the whole world [which at that time was very small, and Egypt the first country to come to the front and actually rule the world during the reign of the Pharaohs]. God conferred on Pharaoh the greatest possible blessing, sending His two best preachers, Moses and Aaron, to proclaim the everlasting Gospel in his royal presence. "God is not mocked," neither does He mock anybody. All His words and ways are sincerity, truth and righteousness. His purpose in reference to Pharaoh was his conversion to the Christianity of his dispensation, as he actually owned all the men and money in the world in the capacity of absolute universal monarch. If he had been converted to God, he was the very man to send the Gospel to every human home beneath the skies, thus "proclaiming God's name in all the earth." The simple conclusion follows, as a legitimate sequence, that Pharaoh, like every other sinner, defeated the purpose of God by his own haughty rejection of His loving mercy, thus bringing on himself terrible calamities in this world, and plunging into an eternity of woe.

I have often looked this very man in the face. When you visit Egypt you will find his mummified body in the Gizet Museum. He is a perfect specimen of human symmetry, about six feet tall, and one hundred and eighty pounds weight, and his royal physiognomy showing up gigantic intellect.

CHAPTER II.

THE POTTER AND THE CLAY.

Rom. 9:21-23: "Had not the potter power over the clay of the same lump to make one vessel unto honor, and another unto dishonor? But if God, wishing to show forth his wrath and make his power known, has endured with much long-suffering the vessels of wrath which have been perfected unto destruction, and in order to make known the riches of His glory in behalf of the vessels of mercy, which he has before prepared for his glory. . . ."

This is regarded as an impregnable battering-ram against the doctrine of free grace and universal salvation. The *vox-populi* raises another lugubrious howl, "If God has made me a vessel unto honor, well may all the world salute me, *fortunatus sis O homo* (fortunate art thou, O man); but if He has made me a vessel unto dishonor, alas for me! Infinitely better if I never had been born." While the popular exegesis of this Scripture shows up vividly the elect and the non-elect, upon a fair and simple investigation of the passage, you will see not an insinuation involved, which is out of harmony with free grace and the glorious possibility of universal salvation.

(*b*) N. B.—The word in this passage correctly translated "honor" is *timee,* and has no meaning but financial remuneration. This conclusion is sustained by universal lexical and critical authority. Where Paul says, "Let the elders who preside dutifully be considered worthy of double honor, especially those who labor in the word and doctrine," the simple meaning is double financial remuneration. Now, with this fact before us, let us analyze the problem of the potter and the clay. Our work is signally facilitated by the fact that ancient pottery has survived the ages unchanged down to the present day. I have my mind on a pottery in Madison County, Kentucky, operated by a Methodist preacher of my intimate acquaintance. In every case the potter aims to make a financial success, regardless of the size, shape or character of the vessel he manufactures. Never in all the world did a potter set out to make a dishonorable vessel, from the simple fact that such a vessel is utterly spoiled in the *modus operandi*, and he loses his time and material, making not a cent of money. The only reason why he makes the spoiled vessel is because, having done his best, the clay mars in his hands, and the job proves an utter failure, fit only for the ditches. He cannot put it on his land, as it will sterilize and ruin it. Therefore he is constrained to toss it into the heap of rubbish, whence it will be hauled away and dumped into the ditches. Now, how would this apply to the Omnipotent Potter? You see the analolgy clearly enforces the conclusion that God always sets out to make a good man. It would be the work of Satan to make any other. Then, as He is omnipotent, why does He not always succeed? Who can contravene His power? Of course, the answer is positively negative, so far as potentiality is concerned. Now, seeing that the Omnipotent Potter every time undertakes to make a vessel unto honor, why does He ever fail and make one unto dishonor? The answer to this puzzle is found in the human symbolism. You see the human potter always aims to make a paying job, doing his utmost to steer clear of failure and bankruptcy. But despite all he can do, the clay mars in his hands and the vessel is spoiled and the job a failure. He makes no money, but loses all. Now, you see, when we make the application to the Omnipotent Potter, we must find some thing in the material homogeneous to the marring of the clay in the potter's hands. Now what is it? Indubitably it is intrinsical in humanity. Therefore it must be something disharmonious with the Divine will and character. Rom. 8:7: "The carnal mind is enmity against God, not subject to his law, neither indeed can be." This is the only disharmony between God's will and character. Therefore, while God is going ahead with His glorious, beneficent work, making a good man, truly by philosophers denominated "the noblest work of God," behold, as in case of the human potter when he is doing his best to make a satisfactory, salable vessel, which will command good money in market, despite his utmost efforts the clay mars and, instead of making a marketable vessel, he simply makes another accession to the already distressing heap of spoiled vessels, fit only to be cast into the abyss. Hence you see the application to the Omnipotent Potter simply involves the conclusion that, while God is doing His best to make a good man, *i. e.*, a vessel unto honor, the material mars in His hands, *i. e.*, the human will, dominated by carnality, antagonizes the will of God, thus irremediably contravening the beneficent enterprise of the Omnipotent Potter and superinducing his own dreadful doom of ejectment into the waste pile, destined to an eternity of disappointment, failure discomfiture and despair.

(*c*) The word "fitted" in that awful adjunct, "fitted to destruction," is *kateer tismena*, is the perfect passive participle from *katar tizoo*, to perfect, hence we see an actual perfection for damnation antithetical to the Christian perfection for heaven. In this probation we are all swinging between the two opposite poles of destiny's battetry, the perfect elimination of carnality or spirituality. Verily, every soul is constantly ripening for an eternity of bliss or woe. It is the purpose of the Omnipotent Potter to make us all vessels of honor, non-forfeitable, forever. But He is not going to contravene that glorious freedom which contradistinguishes us from the animal creation, even in order to keep us out of an endless hell. The simple solution of eternity's great problem is the fact that we

ELECTION AND PREDESTINATION. 13

all verify the old Latin proverb, *"Quisque Suae fortunae* ("Every one the architect of his own fortune"), i. e., we make our own heaven or hell and carry it in us through all eternity. In case the Omnipotent Potter really has His way, we will all certainly prove vessels of honor, as Omnipotence actually finds no hard jobs. Yet such is His respect for the autocracy with which He has honored humanity that He will never contravene it, even to keep us out of hell, but let us alone in our sovereign independency to walk deliberately into the burning pit. We see in this passage the doctrine of perfection clearly revealed, both in the appertinency to the righteous and the wicked, precisely as the former ripened for heaven, the latter mature for damnation.

(d) The removal of the clay out of the bank into the pottery is the conversion of the soul from the kingdom of Satan into the realm of grace. The elimination of all unworkable material out of the clay, subsequent to its transportation from the bank into the pottery, constitues he second work, *i. e.,* sanctification. Then follows the manipulations on the potter's lathe, transforming the vessel pursuant to the wisdom and skill of the potter, which in the realm of experience constitutes that great and important work of character building. In all this the vessel must be completely at the option of the potter, to manipulate it *ad libitum,* turning it withersoever he will. Sometimes it is in the sunshine, sometimes under water. It is his prerogative to grind it up *ad libitum* and again spread it out on his lathe for another manipulation. It makes, literally, no difference in what condition we may chance to be, if we are only in the hands of the Potter. He is certain to manage us all right. This character-building is the great period of the entire *modus operandi,* and constitutes that period of Christian experience significantly denominated "growth in grace." After the transformation work is all complete and the spoiled vessels hauled away and dumped into the ditches, there still remains an important work to be administered by the Potter, and that is the ornamentation. Here he has an endless variety of vessels, exhibiting all conceivable shapes and sizes, thus magnifying the wisdom of the potter. In the grand finale of his ingenious and faithful manipulations of these endless varieties constituting his stock in trade, the final delicate though indispensable work of ornamentation supervenes.

(e) Justification takes away the condemnation superinduced by our own transgressions when the Holy Ghost gives us a new heart and gives us citizenship in the kingdom. Sanctification takes away original sin, gives us Christian perfection and wedlock with the Lord, *i. e.,* membership in the bridehood, thus gloriously adapting us to the glorification of God in this life. Yet all this leaves us full of infirmities liable to do wrong, aiming to do right, still exposed to the humiliation of multitudinous mistakes, which can only be re-

ELECTION AND PREDESTINATION. 15

lieved by glorification when this mortal shall put on immortality. This final great work of the Holy Ghost confers on us angelic perfection, which we must have in order to go up and live in heaven with the unfallen angels, who have never known sin nor sorrow and are, consequently, free from mistakes. To the extent of their prerogative they know perfectly so as to be free from the embarrassment of mistakes and blunders. These infirmities are not sins, but the scars which sin in its cruel lacerations has left upon the soul. Yet they need the atoning blood. In the former dispensation they are vividly symbolized by the cities of refuge, representing Christ, the Deliverer of the unwitting homicides who slays a person accidentally, and would certainly be slain outright by the avenger of blood if the offender did not reach the city of refuge. These were six, three on either side of the Jordan; on the west, Keedesh, in Galilee; Shechem, in Samaria, and Hebron, in Judea. On the east, Ramoth, in Rueben; Golon, in Gad, and Bezer, in the south. Every Israelite had his eye on the most convenient city of refuge, ready thither to fly in case of unwitting homicide. Though by the hardest running he barely escapes the sword of the avenger till he can fall through the gate into the city of refuge, he is then perfectly safe, as the avenger is certain not to hurt him, even though flying with an incorrigible impetuosity which precipitates him on the exhausted and prostrate fugitive, the avenger is sure not to hurt him, as in case he should kill him, even accidentally, he would be in the same awful dilemma, pursued by the consanguinity of his victim, hot on his track. This great third work of the Holy Ghost, denominated glorification, takes place when this mortal puts on immortality.

(*f*) As sanctification is the last work of grace we can receive, pursuant to our own volition, glorification being the normal prerogative of the sanctified, not received by faith, but normally conferred by the Holy Ghost as the legitimate sequence of sanctification, therefore all third experiences as an object of our seeking, reception and oppropriation in this life, are illusory and conducive to fanaticism and detrimental to victorious Christian experience. This follows as a logical sequence from the fact that sanctification is really the great experience, absorbing all others and abiding forever, even glorification, its normal sequence, proving only its beautiful and eternal concomitant.

(*g*) I was reared in a wild, mountainous country, where wild animals roamed through the forests, and among them wild chickens. Often, when out in the woods hunting our stock, or laboring, my attention has suddenly been arrested by the violent barking of my dog or the cackling of a hen which he had stirred up. I see her flying so low down as to enthuse the dog with the immediate assurance of catching her in his wide-open mouth, as he darts after her at locomotive speed. Sometimes she even drops down on the ground and runs a while, in order to intensify his already thrilling anticipation of taking her in his mouth every moment; consequently he dashes along at breakneck speed, every moment thinking she is his victim; when suddenly, having decoyed him so far from her fugitive chicks, all this time hidden in the leaves, as to insure their safety, she now leaps up on a tree and takes a good rest. The dog, faint with fatigue, barks a little while, gives up in despair and goes on with his master. Now that all danger is over, she goes back to her chicks, clucks them up, and to her infinite joy counts every one. I give this vivid illustration of Satan's fond trickery, devising the third blessing of "power," "fire," "tongues," or something else, utilized as an adroit stratagem to decoy the Holiness people away from sanctification, the grand *sine qua non*, "without which no one shall see the Lord" (Heb. 12:14). Here we see in this problem of salvation illustrated by the pottery the third work of grace, constituting the gloss which the potter imparts to all of his vessels to make them shine with supernatural beauty, radiance and splendor.

N. B.—The vessels are complete without it, yet they lack the beauty which the finishing touch of fascinating investiture alone can impart. Though the vessels are complete without it, and will answer every purpose, yet the beautiful shine thus imparted is not to be depreciated. Now, reader, if you can see anything in all of this transaction of the potter and the clay out of harmony with free grace, I must give you credit for extraordinary optical dynamics.

CHAPTER III.

JACOB AND ESAU.

Rom. 9:11: "For the children not having been born nor done anything good or evil, in order that the purpose of God might stand according to election, not of works, but of him that calleth, it is said to her that the elder shall serve the younger; moreover, it has been written, Jacob have I loved and Esau have I hated." . . . . It is pertinent that we here simply note the lapse of six hundred years before Malachi wrote this commendation of Jacob and condemnation of Esau, many centuries after they had both passed away, the prophet simply using those names representative of nationalities which so differentiated either from other as to evoke the blessing of God on Israel, His Holy people, and the righteous anathema against the Edomites, the children of Esau, who were a wicked, idolatrous people. In the differentiation of these rival boys over the patrimony of their father, a millionaire, because he had inherited the unbroken estate of his father Abraham, whom God had wonderfully blessed

ELECTION AND PREDESTINATION. 19

with boundless wealth, both temporal and spiritual, we recognize a new species of election and predestination hitherto unseen, as the two preceding arguments appertaining to the election of grace, which is perfectly free, always has been and always will be, from the fact that grace means free and unmerited favor. Therefore you can rest assured that salvation and heaven have always been free for every son and daughter of Adam's ruined race, and always will be. This, the gracious economy, irrevocably guarantees to every human being. Our Lord's valedictory invitation, "Whosoever will, let him come and take the water of life freely"—this is the proclamation of the Spirit and the Bride, *i. e.*, the blessed Holy Ghost, the Spirit of the Father and the Son, and the Bride of Christ, *i. e.*, His blood-washed Church. Our great work and glorious privilege is thus to co-operate with the Holy Ghost in ringing out the invitation to all the ends of the earth, "Come, drink the water of life freely, without money and without price." While there never can be any defalcation appertaining to the election of grace, which Peter certifies is "through the sanctification of the Spirit and belief of the truth, in conversion we are nominated, in sanctification we are elected, and in glorification we are crowned kings and queens to reign forever.

William Henry Harrison was elected President of our Republic in 1844, but lost his life before his inauguration, consequently h never did preside over the United States. In a similar manner truly sanctified people may go down in the battle with Satan, thus forfeiting spiritual life before the transfiguration glory inaugurates them into the eternal, triumphant reign with Christ.

(*h*) N. B.—While the election of grace is conditional upon perfect and external submission to God, and the heroic faith which really takes Christ for everything, bringing the shout of victory into the soul to abide forever, in the above Scripture we strike a radically different line of election, *i. e.*, the divine progenitorship which was attended with many and great blessings, *e. g.*, the identity with the immediate consanguinity of Jesus and custodianship of the divine oracles, normally accompanied by the prophetical schools of the different ages. Thus many vast and incalculable blessings accompanied this Messianic progenitorship. In the house of Noah there was an election with reference to the Messianic progenitorship. Shem was elected, Ham and Japheth were reprobated, yet Christ died for them as truly as for Shem. Eventually there was another election in the house of Terah; Abraham was elected and all the balance of the world reprobated; Isaac was elected and Ishmael reprobated; then in the house of Isaac, Jacob was elected and Esau reprobated. In the family of Jacob, Judah was elected and the other nine tribes reprobated. It was absolutely necessary that the world should have an unbroken predecession of the divine progenitorship running all the way back to Adam, so as forever to establish the great historic fact that Jesus is the veritable son of Adam and, consequently, competent to represent all of Adam's race and thus take our place under the violated law. In this Messianic progenitorship we have the consolation of three Gentile mothers of our Lord, *i. e.*, Thamar, the daughter-in-law of Judah, Rahab of Jericho, in the E. V. denominated the harlot, but as you see in my version, the female tavern-keeper, which is the primary meaning of the Hebrew *zonah*. It is not probable that Joshua's godly spies, sent over to Jericho, stopped at a house of ill-fame. That they put up at a tavern which happened to be kept by a woman was not at all improbable. When Israel took the city and possessed the country, this woman wedded an Israelitish man, whose name was Salmon. God gave them a son, whom they named Boaz. He became the husband of Ruth, the Moabitess, and God gave them a son, Obed, the father of Jesse, the father of David, the father of Jesus. Hence you see our Lord had three Gentile mothers in His progenitorship, quite consolatory to all of us Gentiles to know that Jesus is really our own consanguinity. While this election to the Messianic progenitorship is the most glorious honor ever conferred on mortals, and attended with privileges and blessings innumerable and invaluable, and in its very nature absolute and unconditional, chosen of God from all eternity, yet it is not an election to heaven, neither does its reprobation involve damnation, because Christ died for every human being of all ages and nations, and brought salvation within their reach, whereas only a little sprinkle, comparatively participated in pre-Messianic election.

(*i*) The reason why the controversy between Jacob and Esau was so hot, and continues even to the present day, was because Esau, according to patriarchal law, which gave the first-born a double portion of their father's estate, was really entitled to the birthright. Jacob and his mother, who was in deep sympathy with him, apprehensive of this fact, resorted to a series of stratagems in order to secure the birthright for him, despite the force of patriarchal law. In this they were unfortunate, taking trouble on themselves and even committing sin gratuitously, because God had settled that matter and already given the progenitorship to Jacob, hence the stratagem he ran on his hungry brother, inducing him to sell his birthright for a mess of pottage, in an hour when he was dying of hunger, and in his youth, had no clear apprehension of the value of his birth-right, and legitimately concluded that it would be worthless to him if he never lived to enjoy the double portion of his father's estate. Therefore he sold it out for a mess of pottage, thus provoking the ridicule of the world, as they all mock his folly. Yet every sinner on the globe really does the same

ELECTION AND PREDESTINATION. 23

thing, *i. e.*, sells his birthright for pottage, thus feeding his body and starving his soul to death. While Esau delayed with his venison which he was to bring his father, that he might eat, revive and bless him, Jacob, pursuant to the manipulations of the mother, who cooked the kid tender and savory and put on him Esau's goatskin gloves, as he was a hairy man, and Jacob smooth, and entering the tent after nightfall and mimicking Esau's voice, says, "Arise, my father, and eat of thy son's venison and bless me." The father responds, "Art thou my son Esau?" He answers in the affirmative. Then he says, "Come nigh unto me, that I may put my hand on thee and know that thou art verily my son Esau." Then he replies, when he puts his hands upon the hairy goatskin gloves which Rebecca had put on Jacob: "It is truly the voice of Jacob, but the hands of Esau." As Jacob had done his best to counterfeit his brother's voice, and had partially succeeded, now in confirmation of the feeling concludes that he is really Esau, and proceeds to bless him. So Jacob, having received the blessing, retreats with all possible expedition, leaving his father really impressed that he has given Esau the blessing as he intended. Scarcely have the echoes of his retreating feet ceased to reverberate when Esau arrives with the venison and says: "Arise, my father, and eat of your son's venison, and bless me." Then the old man, astounded beyond measure, wakes up to the delusion that has already been played on him. Now the secret is out, and the whole matter is clear. Jacob has successfully played Esau on his father. Now Esau lifts up his voice with a loud, bitter cry, and proceeds to importune his father, despite the fraud thus practiced by his brother, to revoke the blessing and confer it on him. Here is where Esau's repentance (Heb. 12 ch.) comes in. It says that he "sought repentance and found it not, though he earnestly sought it with tears."

(j) Repentance, *meta noia*, from *meta*, change, and *noos*, the mind, literally means simply a change of mind. In Christian experience it means to get rid of the carnal mind and receive the mind of Christ. Here it does not mean a repentance in the heart of Esau, as that was not the thing he sought, but a repentance on the part of his father, in which he would change his mind, revoke the blessing from Jacob and confer it on him. This his father could not do, as God had already settled the matter that Jacob was to have it. The *vox populi* lifts up the sympathetic wail of Esau and condoles his awful fate with flowing tears, seeking repentance and finding it not, because he was reprobated. That is all true. But the whole matter had nothing to do with Esau's personal salvation, but simply the progenitorship of Christ to which Jacob was elected before he was born and from which Esau was reprobated. But this election had nothing to do

ELECTION AND PREDESTINATION. 25

with the salvation of either. Jacob was not in that matter elected to heaven. [He received that election when sanctified on the bank of the Jabbok, twenty-two years subsequently.] Neither was Esau reprobated to damnation, and we have no record that he *ever* was; but he was simply reprobated from the Messianic progenitorship, which had nothing to do with personal salvation or damnation. Christ died for Esau and the Edomites, his children, as truly as for Jacob and the Israelites, his children. When, twenty-two years subsequently, Jacob spent that night with God on the bank of the Jabbok, wrestling till the break of day, the Lord meanwhile demanding his name, which he was so reluctant to give. Of course *He* knew his name, but if we want His blessing we must all confess our depravity, overtly and unequivocally. Jacob means *rascal,* as Hebrew words are all significant. Jacob had to confess his rascality and turn over the rascal (old Adam) to the Lord to slay him. The moment he makes the confession the Lord slays the rascal revealing it, by dislocating his thigh, the symbol of strength, thus typifying the crucifixion of "old Adam." Now he crosses the Jabbok as the sun rises and goes on the way his people and their herds and flocks had preceded him the preceding day. Now he meets his brother, who runs to him, they mutually embrace, kiss and bless. From the notable transaction and fraud practiced in the patriarchal tent twenty-two years antecedently, Esau had cherished unrelenting animosity, resolving to kill his brother on sight, thus constraining him to become a fugitive for his life. Forced to dash away with only a staff for a companion, he runs all night and all the next day, imagining that he hears the tread of his infuriated brother on his heels ready to kill him. The second night of his flight, faint with fatigue, Jacob falls down on Mt. Bethel, with a stone for his pillow, and the constellations his chandelier, and the howl of the wild beast the only music to lull him into slumber. Sheer weariness wraps him in the mantle of *somnus*. Meanwhile God blesses him with a heavenly vision. He sees the ladder resting on *terra firma* and reaching the glittering constellations, on which glorified angels come down and sanctified pilgrims climb up. Amid these heavenly visions his soul receives a touch from the Almighty, and inspiration articulates, "Surely this is none other than the house of God and the gate of heaven." There originated the name of that notable mountain which, with others, I have repeatedly trodden. *Beth* means house and *el*, God, not a building, but a family; as we say, "the house of Abraham," knowing that he never did live in a house, but always in a tent. Hence we see in this notable heavenly vision his soul was converted, and he became a member of God's family. Twenty-two years have rolled away; he has toiled hard and suffered much, and God has blessed him spiritually and temporally, and he has become

ELECTION AND PREDESTINATION. 27

a millionaire. His great second blessing, on the bank of the Jabbok, is denominated Peniel, from *peni,* face, and *el,* God, because there he saw the face of God. Though we have only the inspired history of Jacob that memorable night, the corroborative facts clearly indicate and warrant the conclusion that Esau spent that wonderful night with God, as well as his brother, whereas he had come to meet him with four hundred men to kill him, when he saw him, oblivious to all the old animosities, he runs to meet him, embraces and kisses him, with the congratulatory shout, "O, my brother, I see you, as the face of an angel, after so many long years!" But a critic says the ten-thousand-dollar present which Jacob had sent on to meet him had appeased his wrath, mitigated his fury, and transformed him into a lovely, friendly brother. This is hardly tenable, from the simple fact that he positively declined to accept it. In truth, God had wonderfully blessed Esau in temporal things, as well as Jacob, making him a prince in the land and giving him boundless wealth. He said to Jacob, "My brother, keep these valuable presents, for I have enough." But when Jacob begged him to accept it all as a souvenir of his brotherly love, of course he could not decline. Suffice it to say that notable meeting wound up the lifelong controversy between the brothers. They became firm friends and so remained till the close of their lives. I verily believe Esau spent that wonderful night of blessing with God, so prominently chronicled in the life of Jacob, on the bank of the Jabbok, while Jacob and Esau wound up their controversy in that memorable meeting which has been memorialized by the returning Jews, who have erected a beautiful city on the spot [Synadelphia—meeting of the brothers], which God permitted me to see in 1899; the old controversy was perpetuated by their children, and has never yet gone down, the Turks, the children of Esau, this day holding the land of Canaan with the grip of a drowning man, on the allegation that it belongs to them according to the Abrahamic covenant, pursuant to the patriarchal law, which gave the first-born a double portion of the father's estate, and in verification of their hereditary rights, the children of Esau, with a tight grip, are determined to hold it forever. Meanwhile the children of Jacob from the ends of the earth pouring in, determined to recover the land bequeathed to them by the Abrahamic covenant.

(k) N. B.—While the election to the Messianic progenitorship is unconditional and irreversible, it has nothing to do with personal salvation, and never did; yet it is exceedingly prominent in the Bible. Therefore, when you read about election and predestination, always from the context settle the matter whether it is the election of grace or the divine progenitorship. If you will diligently settle that one problem, and thus relieve all your perplexity on the subject of election and non-election, predestination and reprobation, perfectly rely on the conclusion that the unconditional election all simply appertains to the Messianic progenitorship, having nothing to do with personal salvation and never did; meanwhile all the election of grace is perfectly free for every son and daughter of Adam's race, without a solitary exception. Appertaining to the election of grace, Sam Jones pertinently said that the elect of man is will, and the non-elect the man that will not.

CHAPTER IV.

GOD'S IPSIC DIXIT COMPATIBLE WITH THE HUMAN WILL.

In confirmation we see a notable case in the history of David's seven-year flight from Saul, pursuing him everywhere like the partridge, over mountain and dale, through forest and vale, to kill him, suspicious that he would one day supplant him and his dynasty in the kingdom. Meanwhile David and his six hundred men come to Keilah and find the city and province in deep distress on account of the frequent raids made by the Philistines robbing their threshing floors and driving away their herds and flocks, thus impoverishing the land. This inspired history you find in 1 Sam. 23d chapter. David comes to the relief, fights and conquers the Philistines, delivering the country of the distressing nuisance, until universal peace reigned and prosperity returned. Of course the Kahaelites are making all the world of David and his men who had so gloriously delivered them from their troublesome enemies. Because David, in his early flight from Saul, went to the city of Knol and the priests in the succession of Melchisedec received him kindly. Saul had them all slain, except Abialthes, the son of Ahimelec, their leader, who fled away, joined David and remained with him to the end of his life. He had with him the ephod, which contained those beautiful precious stones through which they consulted the Lord, who gave answer through these urim and thumin, by radiation and flashes of light emanating from them. While the Kelites are manifested all conceivable appreciation of David and his men, he thought it safe to consult the Lord whether Saul would come to Keilah; in case he did come, whether the Kelites would deliver him up, thus purchasing royal favor with their heads. When he thus propounds to the God of Israel these important questions, will Saul come down to Keilah? the answer comes promptly from heaven, He will come down to Keilah. Then David propounds the other transcendently important question, Will the men of Keilah deliver me up? To this the divine response follows promptly, They will deliver thee up. If David had believed hackneyed dogma,

ELECTION AND PREDESTINATION. 31

what is to be will be, and if a man is born to die by the fall of a tree, he will go that way, though he may never be in the woods, he would have put his face between his hands, raised the lugubrious howl and given up to die without an effort. But he had a better acquaintance with God than some of our modern predestinarians. He understood distinctly, Saul will come down if I stay here, and if I am here when he comes the men of Keilah will deliver me up. Consequently he seizes his trumpet and blows a double-quick march with all his might, saying to his men: Saul is coming and these Kelites for whom we have fought and delivered at the peril of our lives, and who have poured on us floods of flattery, will turn against us and purchase royal favor with our heads. Consequently he bids them all march a double-quick toward the rising sun, whereas Saul was pursuing him from the north, by his scouts keeping constantly posted with reference to David's movements. Therefore when Saul heard that David was gone from Keilah he changed his course, striking off on the hypothenuse of a right angled triangle in a southeasterly direction to intercept David. Now you see, whereas God said to David, Saul will come down to Keilah and the men of Keilah will deliver thee up, you see neither of those wills ever took place, from the simple fact that David and his men fled away and Saul did not come and David was not there for them to deliver even if he had come. Hence you see the Bible is chucked full of solid common sense and not a scintilla of foolishness from lid to lid. Neither are there any contradictions in the Bible. That is the reason why we all ought to have a correct translation of the Bible in plain English, as even our salvation depends on it.

(*l*) As you see from the clear and notable case of Keilah that the change of David's position kept Saul from coming and of the facts involved confirmed the conclusion that when God said He will come down to Keilah, a subjunctive clause was understood, and that was, if David stayed there. You plainly see, from David's deportment, he understood it in that way, and when he said, The men of Keilah will deliver thee up, a subjunctive was clearly implied involving the complexed dependent adjunct, If you stay and Saul comes, they will deliver you up. God makes no mistakes. He was acquainted with God and knew that he would understand, subjoining those conditional clauses. These facts illustrate the importance of not only believing God's Word but retaining our own intelligence and using it faithfully and heroically. Rom 8:29: "Whom he did foreknow, he did also predestinate to be conformed to the image of his son." Here we see a predestination predicated of foreknowledge. It is a sad mistake to identify the two. With God there is no fore-knowledge or after-knowledge, because everything is present with Him. Finite minds cannot comprehend the omnipotence and omnipresence of the Almighty. We get into trouble when we undertake to comprehend God's attributes, which are entirely beyond our powers of interpretation.

N. B.—God's knowledge does not make it so, from the simple fact that knowledge is not influence and consequently does not cause anything. We can approximate these mysteries by the diagnosis of human knowledge, *e. g.,* your son is going headlong into drunkenness and then concomitant debauchery. You know he is going to ruin as fast as he can, but your knowledge of the fact which is bringing down your gray hairs to the grave does not make him expedite down to the bottomless pit. Just like densely populated localities all traversed with roads, so is the ocean. The ship roads across the Atlantic are about thirty miles wide. In the exploration of the ocean along some routes sub-oceanic mountain summits are found, lifting up formidable rocks which knock a hole in every ship that strikes them and let in the thundering sea and precipitate her a dismal wreck down to the oceanic bottom, with all her crew and passengers, there to await the judgment trumpet, responsive to which the sea will give up her dead. Those dangerous routes are definitely marked and sedulously avoided. International law in her courts of admiralty rigidly prohibit any one to serve as pilot who is not thoroughly posted, and in whose hands the ship will not be safe. Now an old pilot, thoroughly acquainted with the

Atlantic Ocean, stands on the wharf at New York and sees the ship sail away. He knows by her bearings that she is on a perilous route and destined to be wrecked, yet his knowledge has nothing to do with bringing about the wreckage. If human knowledge is not influenced, then Divine knowledge is not influenced. In these Scriptures you see that the predestination is predicated of the foreknowledge. God verily knows everything, from beginning to end. While every human being is perfectly free to choose the good and live, or choose the bad and die, yet God knows what every one will do, and appoints the destination accordingly. This is no interference with freedom which operates in a smaller interior circle, while God in His omnipotence knows what every one will choose and do. That knowledge is not appointment, but He makes the oppointment in harmony with His knowledge of their character.

(n) The old Romans had a trite maxim, *Similius similies congregantur* (birds of a feather flock together. While God has elected character, we make our own election by developing those characters. It is very consolatory to the Lord's people to think that He saw and knew us from all eternity, and so wisely and beneficently appointed for us the diversified happy lots with which He has blessed our lives from the beginning, and made them a glorious sunshine. I believe we are all immortal till our work is done.

CHAPTER V.

JUDICIAL REPROBATION.

Matt. 24:22: "And unless those days were shortened, no flesh would be saved; but for the sake of the elect those days will be shortened." Here we have the shortening of the Jewish tribulation [which began A.D. 66 and lasted seven years] for the sake of the elect of Israel. Josephus says that in the siege of Jerusalem, a million of people perished by the sword, pestilence and famine, and ninety thousand were sold in slavery. In the above scripture Jesus predicted the abbreviation of the tribulation period, in order to save the elect of Israel who were there in the siege, and if it had continued, would certainly have perished, because the people died so fast they could not bury them, and the putrefactions developed pestilence which would actually have depopulated the city. These elect of Israel are now gathering from the ends of the earth into the Holy Land, still unconverted, in fulfillment of Ezekiel, ch. 37, where you see the millions of dry bones piled all over that boundless valley, to the whole "house of Israel" He says, "I will bring you up out of your graves and gather you again into your own land." During the long ages of their expatriation and denominationalization they are dispersed among all the nations of the earth, *i. e.*, their nationality buried in all lands. Amid the universal fulfillment of the latter-day prophecies, so vividly ominous of our Lord's near coming, this very day the elect of Israel from every nation under heaven are rising out of their graves, after an interment of eighteen hundred years, and gathering into their own land, from which they have been expatriated ever since their awful tribulation, which robbed them of their nationality and drove them from their earthly inheritance. While this gathering is really wonderful, in flufillment of the prophecy they are still unconverted, *i. e.*, "dry bones" verifying our Savior's *ipse dixit*— "the first shall be last and the last shall be first." We should press the evangelization of all the Gentiles with all possible expedition, as every nation must receive the Gospel (Matt. 24:14) before the King of Israel will return on the throne of His millennial glory and establish His kingdom in all the earth, never to have an end—Dan. 7 ch. When the Lord shall come to take His waiting bride up to the marriage supper of the Lamb, there to abide during the great Gentile tribulation, meanwhile passing through that important adjudication preparatory to her subordinate administration of all nations during the glorious millennial reign. Rev. 20:6: "Blessed and holy is he that hath part in the first resurrection , for over such the second death will have no power, but they shall be kings and priests unto God and reign with Him a thousand years." This thrilling Johanic prophecy indubitably warrants the conclusion that the Lord will rule the world during the millennium, through the instrumentality of His transfigured saints. Therefore the tribulation period utilized on earth in the elimination of the incorrigibles and unsavables, who have reprobated themselves by the blasphemy of the Holy Ghost (Matt. 31:32), *i. e.,* His contemptuous rejection, and thus crossed the dead line. We see these alarming prophecies fulfilled on a grand scale whithersoever we turn our illuminated vision, whether to the Church, plunging headlong into dead formality, hollow hypocrisy and worldly conformity, or to the wicked world, with locomotive speed rushing into skepticism and infidelity. O, how the vast tribulation harvest, already enveloping the globe, is fast ripening for the million of destroying angels (Dan. 7:9), ready to deluge the world with floods of fire, and girdle it with the glittering swords, bristling bayonets and thundering artillery of those Armageddon wars (Rev. 17-19 ch.), destined to deluge the world with blood and heap it with mountains of the slain, thus consummating the awful work of destruction pertinent to the removal of all elements incompatible with the glorious millennial reign, when all nations will "beat their swords into ploughshares and their spears into pruning-hooks," and learn war no more." You have nothing to do but open your eyes and look around and see a world utterly

38 ELECTION AND PREDESTINATION.

unmanageable, by a government of righteous peace, love and holiness, and be assured of the great work to be wrought by Daniel's millions of destroying angels and John's countless myriads of Armageddon soldiers, whose work will simply fulfill the prophecies in the utter removal of the incorrigibles and unsavables.

(o) During the awful tribulation Zechariah tells us in his last chapter that it will sweep over the Holy Land and cut down two-thirds of the Jews who are now gathering thither. When the Lord comes to snatch away His waiting Bride He will wonderfully reveal Himself to His consanguinity, especially the elect of Israel, gathered into the Holy Land and at that time unconverted, *i. e.*, "dry bones" (Ez. 37 ch.). The effect of this revelation will superinduce a wonderful revolutionary evangelization throughout the Hebrew world, and especially the Holy Land. When the Lord takes away His Bride (Dan. 12 ch.) the tribulation will at once set in, and anti-Christ, the Pope, the eighth head of the Roman beast, now the seventh (Rev. 13 ch. and 17 ch.) will at once arise and usurp all the thrones of the world now vocated by the fallen kings (Dan. 7:9). As the Jews are even now working on the temple in Petersburg, Moscow, Berlin, Vienna, London, Paris, Rome and Naples; as Solomon had all the materials prepared in the quarries, Mt. Lebanon and other localities and transported to Jerusalem, just ready to put every piece

ELECTION AND PREDESTINATION. 39

in its place without the sound of hammer or the clangor of the saw, in a similar manner the children of Abraham, in their world-wide dispersions, are now preparing the most valuable materials for the rebuilding of the temple. They have very largely already gotten possession of the land, and will soon have it all in their own hands. Then they will bring in the materials and rebuild the temple. The "man of lawlessness (2 Thess. 2 ch.) is the Pope, the seventh head of the Roman beast; Cæsar, who sat upon the throne of the world in Paul's day, being the sixth head. As the beast can only have one head at a time, Cæsar had to fall before the Pope could take his place. The Goths, Huns, Vandals and Heruli, the ancestors of great Russia, after a three-hundred-years' war for the gold and silver which Rome had spoliated from all nations in her conquests of seven hundred and fifty-three years, and gathered into her metropolis, so the Emperor actually lived in a golden house and looked out on five thousand senators living in silver houses, co-operating with him in the government of the whole world, finally, under the leadership of Attala the Great, captured Rome, A.D. 476, and spent a whole week gathering the gold and silver from the palaces, temples and shrines, common soldiers actually becoming millionaires, after which they returned home bearing their princely fortunes, leaving vacant the throne which the Pope, the seventh head of the beast, ascended. Rev. 17 ch. shows clearly the identity of the eighth head, who will be the anti-Christ of the tribulation, with the seventh who has *been* ani-Christ ever since he succeeded the fallen Emperor, but will be anti-Christ magnified and in the succession of all the fallen kings really claiming the whole world during the tribulation. You see in that (chapter 2, 2 Thess.) an unnamed antagonism to this notable "man of lawlessness," keeping him from rising and taking the place which he so ardently coveted. That place was the Papacy, which he could not take till Cæsar fell, as the world could not have a Cæsar and a Pope both at the same time. Cæsar would have killed the Pope; therefore he could not rise till the barbarian armies shook the Pope down from his throne (A.D. 476). When the Lord takes away His Bride, Daniel 7:9, "I saw till the thrones were cast down and the Ancient of Days did sit, and the fiery stream went before Him, and a thousand thousand [*i. e.*, a million] destroying angels ministered unto him." Here the blessed Father verifies the promise He made His Son when He ascended up from the bloody fields of Calvary, and He hails Him, "Welcome, well done, thou hast bought back that lost world by thy blood; it is thine alone, forever and ever. Sit thou down on my right hand till I make thine enemies thy footstool." He is still sitting there; but pursuant to the wonderful fulfillment of all the prophecies, I am this day expecting the blessed Father to verify His promise, descend from heaven and execute righteous judgments against the wicked nations and fallen churches throughout the whole world, shaking down every usurper, political and ecclesiastical and then vacating every throne beneath the skies for the rightful occupancy of His once humiliated but now exalted Son, our Prophet, Priest and King, the legitimate Heir of every throne, sceptre and diadem, when unfallen angels, archangels, cherubim, seraphim and all the heavenly hierarchies and transfigured saints will crown Him King of kings and Lord of lords to reign forever and ever.

(p) As you see in this chapter (2 Thess. 2), anti-Christ exalts himself above everything which is called God and divinity, sitting in the temple of God and showing himself off that he is God. Meanwhile those Armageddon wars will sweep over the Holy Land and verify Zechariah in the destruction of two-thirds of the Jews gathered thither from the ends of the earth [as election is always twofold]. Even now a great election is gathering the children of Abraham out of all nations. But there must be another. In the kingdom of grace, regeneration elects every citizen out of the devil's kingdom and adopts him into the family of God. Then sanctification elects the Bride of Christ out of God's kingdom. In a similar manner the elect of Israel, for whose sake their awful tribulation was shortened, are now being gathered out of all nations into the Holy Land; but out of them the terrible castigatory judgments of

God in the awful tribulation will consummate another election, evoking the true and the tried who shall have passed through all the appalling fiery trials to which they will be exposed by anti-Christ and his world-encircling millions, who will do everything in their power to bring into conservatism every soul left on the earth in the glorious rapture of the saints, who will enjoy the marriage supper of the Lamb while the forty-five years with which Dan. 12:13 measures the tribulation are doing their momentous work, eliminating all the unsavables and incorrigibles out of every nation under heaven, preparatory to the greatest heavenly harvest that the ages have ever known, awaiting the glorious millennial reign, when all the transfigured saints will be utilized by the Great King in the evangelization of the thronging millions who, in God's infallible providence, will have survived the terrible judgments, whose province it will be to vindicate the Divine administration against all the maladministrations during the roll of six thousand years, superinduced by Satan and his myrmidons. This second election, which will take place among the Jews during the tribulation, will result in the equipment of the surviving third for the most honor ever conferred on human beings, *i. e.*, the service of our Lord's reception committee, when He shall ride down on the throne of His millennial glory, accompanied by the transfigured saints of His Bridehood, now thoroughly organized, every

ELECTION AND PREDESTINATION. 43

one in his place and all ready for the fields of labor which await them in the capacity of prophets, priests and kings, subordinated to and co-operative with His glorious Majesty, as

"He shall have dominion o'er river, sea and shore,
Far as the eagle's pinion or dove's light wing can soar."

This tested and tried survival of the Jewish nation, now serving as our Lord's reception committee, will enjoy the honor of crowning Him King of the Jews, to sit on the throne of His Father David and reign over the house of Jacob forever.

CONCLUSION.

(*q*) The great creeds of Christendom, Calvinian and Arminian, have confronted each other, heroically flashing the controversial sword in the bright light of the glorious Sun of Righteousness, radiated from the inspired Word, the last six thousand years, multiplied millions of preachers and theologians cultured in the didactic theology of these great creedistic hemispheres constituting the luminous globe of Biblical theology. Suffice it to say the end of the age and our Lord's glorious appearing are too nigh for us to waste time in theological tournaments, while the harvest is so great, and efficient laborers so few. While hyper-Calvinism and ultra-Arminianism normally diverge away to opposite poles of the theological battery, let us remember low Calvinism and high Arminianism actually meet on intermediate ground, shake hands, fraternize and mutually bless, arm in arm working together to save a lost world.

N. B.—"It does not behoove the man of God to strive." The word translated *strive* is *machesthai,* to fight a battle. While we are heroically to antagonize for "the faith once delivered to the saints" (Jude 3), we are forbidden to engage in logomachies, *i. e.,* word wars. That word in Jude translated "contend" reveals the awful battle which the gladiator in the Coliseum fought for his life. As we know, he brought into availability all the powers of spirit, mind and body, as his antagonist was liable to kill him every moment. While we are thus commanded to bring into availability all our ransomed powers in this terrible battle with the world, the flesh and Satan, on whose momentous issue kingdoms and crowns are pending, yet we are commanded not to strive in logomachies, but to be gentle and competent to our adversaries, ever sanguinely hopeful that God in His condescending mercy, will grant unto them repentance unto life. Now do we reconcile these two flatly contradictory commandments? It is very simple and easy; while we are never to flicker an iota nor surrender a solitary syllable of the truth, but to verify the Baptist missionary motto, "An ox standing between the plow and the altar, ready for sacrifice or service," not caring whether he pulls the plow or bleeds on the altar, and we are always to be ready to hasten to the firing line,

ELECTION AND PREDESTINATION. 45

and if a martyr is needed, to put in the first bid; yet we are to do all in a meek, lowly and uncontroversial spirit, overflowing with love for those who differ from us, and constantly verifying Epaphras' definition of Christian perfection (Col. 4 ch.) : "Havink been fully carried away in the whole will of God, and more so now than ever," a wonderful definition of this great experience given by Paul's boy preacher. I dare not withhold a solitary syllable of God's truth, lest I lose my soul. I must heroically use God's glittering sword, sparing nothing, but cutting off theological heads right and left, being fully assured that God is ready to give each decapitated trunk a better head than he ever had before, so that he will forever call me blessed for the decisive amputation which the Spirit used me to administer in the gladiatorial exercise of the faithful pulpit.

(r) So few people are really contented to walk alone with an unseen God, which is the only paradise this side the pearly portals. The reason why God permitted the Babylonians to carry Israel into captivity was because, while they all claimed to be true worshippers of the great Jehovah, despite all He could do they would worship other gods also. History wonderfully repeats itself. This day the great majority of the American Church are toiling in spiritual Babylon, groaning over their leanness and bemoaning the dismal dearth in Zion. If they will only put away their strange gods, *i. e.*, ordinances, churchisms, ceremonies, creedisms, water-gods, sacramental gods, and "bring all their tithes into the store-house," and vindicate themselves from the awful crime of robbing God, as the tithe of everything belongs to Him, Malachi assures us He will "pour us out a blessing more than our hearts can contain." Meanwhile the copious overflow will flood the land with salvation on all sides, bringing the lost to God and reviving desolate homes by the shouts of returning prodigals, and fattening starving pilgrims on the fatted calf in every home floating in his own gravy. I am no anti-ordinance preacher; these are beautiful souvenirs of God's redeeming mercy in our wonderful, omnipotent Christ, unstintingly dispensed indiscriminately to submissive, believing souls by the blessed Holy Ghost, sent down from heaven in Pentecostal showers, convicting sinners, regenerating penitents, restoring backsliders, sanctifying believers, and inundating holy pilgrims with His wonderful nine extraordinary gifts, constituting the Christian's panoply, with which we conquer the world, the flesh and Satan, thus bringing down heavenly avalanches and inundating Immanuel's land with heavenly landslides, transforming publicans and sinners, harlots and thieves, into blood-washed and fire-baptized evangelists, proof against ocean storms, railroad wrecks, blood-thirsty cannibals, crocodiles, leopards, lions, tigers, bears, hyenas, smallpox, cholera and bloody persecutions indiscriminately, as they bare their bosoms to the storm and carry the Gospel into the regions beyond, thus heroically expediting our Lord's return to reign in righteousness.

(*s*) The true preventive of all this reckless wasting of our Lord's ammunition in fruitless controversy, Satan's trickery to turn our ammunition away from him, against churches, creeds, doctors and everything else except King Diabolus and his myrmidons, is the baptism of the Holy Ghost and fire, which Jesus gives to all the wholly consecrated, perfectly submissive, eternally abandoned children of God, responsive to meekly receptive and heroically appropriative faith. He gave it to *me* forty years ago, burning up the Freemason, as I was chaplain of the lodge; the Odd Fellow, in whose lodge I also served as chaplain; the college president, the candidate for the Episcopacy, and the Methodist preacher. From that day to this I have never been in the lodge, and have been no more Methodist than some other kind of a preacher; but simply God's mouthpiece, literally dead to everything but His precious Word and sweet will; as dead to Methodism as Campbellism or Romanism, though a member of the Methodist Church all my life, belonging to nothing but God, and constantly sinking deeper into His divinity.

(*t*) N. B.—Follow Jesus, your only Leader, the Holy Ghost, your only Guide, the Bible, especially the New Testament, as we are under that dispensation, your only authority.

Fellowship with the whole Christian world on the basis of the supernatural birth for all sinners, and entire sanctification for all Christians, your charity super-abounding on all non-essentials, while you absolutely make no compromise on the above *sine qua nons*. For these you labor night and day, as without these two great works of the Holy Ghost none will pass the pearly portals. We bewail the sectarian divisions of the Christian world, because they are so detrimental to personal spirituality and so impedimental to the world's evangelization, especially in contemplation of their utter implausibility, from the simple fact that their creeds differentiate wholly on non-essentials, and are consequently without excuse. There is no reason why the whole Christian world should not unite on the supernatural birth for all sinners, and entire sanctification for all Christians, mutually allowing full liberty and extending illimitable charity on non-essentials, all singing and shouting together:

> "Brethren all who disagree,
> And would have charity to please us,
> Union there can never be,
> Unless that we be one in Jesus;
> One as He is one in God,
> In spirit and disposition;
> This the holy Scriptures teach,
> 'Tis plain without an exposition."

Now to the Holiness people in all the earth, regardless of nationality, sect or color, is this book, with its fifty-four predecessors, prayerfully and lovingly dedicated by the author.

Send for Catalogue
OF
Wall Mottoes And Scripture Texts

We import them in a great many beautiful
Designs and Colors
ranging from
5 cents to 75 cents each
Sunday School Reward Cards 25 cents a box containing 12 or 24 cards

They make an inexpensive but artistic decoration for the walls of homes, as well as Sunday-school, Y. M. C. A., and other meeting rooms, and at the same time are silent but effective preachers of the Word.

Liberal Discounts Allowed to Agents

Pentecostal Mission Publishing Company
Nashville, Tenn.

www.ingramcontent.com/pod-product-compliance
Lightning Source LLC
Chambersburg PA
CBHW032113040426
42337CB00040B/547